D0942166

LISTEN
TO THE
TREES

A Poetic Snapshot of West Seattle, Then & Now

◆

Sean Petrie
&
Southwest Seattle Historical Society

DOCUMENTARY MEDIA
SEATTLE
www.docbooks.com

Contents

Introduction

In the summer of 2018, the Southwest Seattle Historical Society teamed up with typing poet Sean Petrie to create on-the-spot poems about and for the residents of the Duwamish peninsula.

For three sun-filled days at the West Seattle Summer Fest, visitors to the Historical Society's booth were asked, "What do you love about West Seattle?"

Folks from age five to eighty-five shared their stories, memories, and favorite things—and then had them turned into original poems, typed then and there, while they watched.

These poems capture a moment in time—the sparkle of West Seattle on those three summer days, the cares and concerns of its residents, and just the sheer bustling joy of the street fair.

But many of the poems also delve into the city's past—odes to cherished places long-gone, ancient advice from its native Duwamish inhabitants, and what it was like growing up in a city so steeped in history. These poems are a tribute to West Seattle, past and present.

Each poem is accompanied by its unique story—a description of the person who requested it, what they asked for a poem about, and why. Each is also presented in its original format—as typed on-the-spot on a 1928 Remington Portable typewriter, mistakes and all.

It's our hope that you will find this collection as authentic, inspiring, diverse, and simply as fun as living in West Seattle itself.

SEAN PETRIE
poet & founder of Typewriter Rodeo

&

SOUTHWEST SEATTLE HISTORICAL SOCIETY

Listen to the Trees

for Ken

One of the visitors to the Historical Society's booth was Ken Workman, the great great great great grandson of Chief Seattle (chief of the Duwamish and Suquamish tribes, the area's indigenous peoples). Ken, who is Duwamish, shared one of his philosophies—that the dead are not entirely powerless, because the trees literally carry the DNA of our ancestors. Which was more than enough inspiration for a poem.

Ken was so moved by his poem that he gave a heartfelt thanks—"Thank you for your writing, thank you for your heart, thank you for your strength"—all spoken in the Duwamish language.

[T]he very dust under your feet ... is the ashes of our ancestors.... [A]nd when your children's children shall think themselves alone in the field ... or in the silence of the woods, they will not be alone.

—Chief Seattle

```
           LISTEN TO THE TREES
                (for Ken)

Want to know
    History?
  Want to hear the dead
        Speak?
  Just pause
   Just plant yourself
     Next to
       A Seattle
         Tree
  Because those roots
      Go deep
        Stretching back
          And down
                Through time
  Touching and tenderly soaking in
     The buried bits
        The literal DNA
          Of all who have come
              Before.
And what will they tell us?
   They will say the dead
      Are not entirely powerless
        That the earth
            Is more loving to our feet
      And to tread carefully
        And respectfully
            And, from time to time,
              Just pause
                And listen
                       To the trees.
```

TOP: Chief Seattle, 1864; BOTTOM: Sean Petrie and Ken Workman, 2018; OPPOSITE: Lincoln Park, 2019

Living History

for Adah

Ever wondered where the beautiful murals that dot the West Seattle walls come from? Longtime resident Adah Cruzen visited the Historical Society's booth and asked for a poetic tribute to her late husband Earl—the man who brought the murals to West Seattle. Adah explained that Earl, while driving around the Sound one day, spotted a mural in another city, and decided that West Seattle needed some of its own. He then made it happen.

The West Seattle murals were commissioned in 1989 to depict various buildings, places, and industries from the area's past. Before even a drop of paint was spilled, the organizers spent over a year researching locations and subjects, and recruiting artists from as far away as Louisiana and Newfoundland.

```
                    LIVING HISTORY
                      (for Adah)
        It may have seemed
           Pretty perfect
              Those West Seattle streets
                 And buildings
                    Back in the day
        But it m took someone
              With a bit more vision
                 And a bit more gumption
                    To jump in his car
                 With some friends
                    Go cruising all around
                       The sound
              And then
                 In that tiny city
                    See those larger than life
                       Works of art
              And to realize
                    YES
                       We need THAT
           And so
              With some friends
                 Some xfxx research and work
                    And of course some paint
              He brought that living history
                 Those outdoor works of xx art
                    To our West Seattle streets.
              And so
                 As you walk by
                    That next great mural
                 Be sure and tip your hat
                    To Earl
                          And say
                             Thanks.
```

Hi-Yu Parade mural, 2019

Alki Beach

for Jessica

Jessica's favorite thing about West Seattle is one that pretty much everyone can relate to. Who hasn't wandered along that historic shore and stopped to gaze at the waves, mountains, and beyond?

```
            ALKI BEACH
               (for Jessica)
No wonder this place
   Was the first
       Those settlers chose --
      Because ▨▨▨▨ here
   Those soft sands
    Soothe your feet
      Those sweeping sea views
        Soothe your soul
   And those ▨▨▨▨ mountains
      Calling in the distance
         Awaken
         Your deepest
         Most majestic
             Dreams...
```

TOP: People looking out from Alki wall, 1940s; BOTTOM: Couple gazing out from Alki, 2019

Active Life

for Emily

Emily loved that living in West Seattle offers so
many opportunities for an active, outdoorsy life.

```
                 ACTIVE LIFE
                  (for Emily)

Sure other cities
  Might claim to be healthy
     Might claim to have the active

          Lifestyle
But
       Take a walk down
           And then up
                From Alki
Have some fresh fish
  At Marination
    Or the salad bar
         At Met Market
And then zip
    Just a few miles away
       For a hike on Mt Si
And you will discover
   Not just what it means
           To live healthy and active
             But just what it means
                 To truly
                     Live.
```

TOP RIGHT: Colman family at camp, holding oars, 1914; BOTTOM: Kayakers on Elliott Bay, 2019

Westward street view from Orleans and Hillcrest, 2019

Walking West Seattle

for Anna

Anna's favorite thing is one many of us share—simply walking the wondrous West Seattle streets. She almost always strolls with her dog, Goldie, and loves to finish their journey with a donut, wherever she can find one.

WALKING WEST SEATTLE
(for Anna)

Where else
   Can you stroll
      From the ~~fathers~~ stores and sights
         Of The Junction
  Walk down
     Those gently
      (And sometimes steeply!)
      Sloping hills
    Past the craftsman houses
    Filled with cozy flowers
     And towering trees
    Where you gently wind your way
       To ~~xx~~ the Alki shore
    Goldie
      Sometimes leading you
      Sometimes sniffing
       At EVERYTHING

Where
   This wonderful walk
   Gets capped off
By perfection:
  The ~~fx~~ soft sweet donut
   In your hand
  That
    Like your West Seattle walk
     Always
       Hits
        The spot.

Walking RR Ave. in the Harbor Ave. business district, 1908

Cars That Go By Themselves

for Freddy

Freddy, one of the youngest visitors to the Historical Society's booth, asked for a poem about "cars that go by themselves."

Maybe he knows a bit more than the rest of us—perhaps he knows that, much like the street trolleys of old, the future of transportation in West Seattle will be vehicles that do the work for you: self-driven cars.

Freddy's Mom: "I honestly don't know where his idea came from for cars that go by themselves, but he was amazed by being able to watch you write it. A week or so later we were at a birthday party and he was playing with a little toy piano. He said it was his typewriter and he went around asking everyone what they wanted a poem about."

Freddy reading his poem, 2018

CARS THAT GO BY THEMSELVES
(for Freddy)

Oh some cars need
A driver and gas
To get anywhere
Either slow or fast

But give me the cars
That do it themselves
They don't need
Fancy whistles or bells

They can move on their own
Even turn and steer
They can zoom by QUICK
Or stay right here

Yup there they go
Those self-moving cars
Of all the vehicles
They're the true -- stars.

West Seattle cable car, 1895

In 1904, West Seattle built an electric streetcar line from the ferry terminal to the intersection of California Avenue and College Street. Because they were much smaller than the trolleys in Seattle, these West Seattle streetcars were often called "the Dinky."

Elliott Bay

for Elliott Bay Brew Pub

On a break during the street fair typing, Sean wrote this as an ode to his favorite gathering place in West Seattle—the Elliott Bay Brew Pub. It's still displayed on the bar.

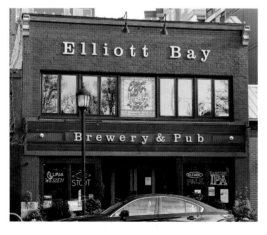

```
                    ELLIOTT BAY

        Just settle in
             To one of those well-worn stools
        Just find your place
                  At the bar
             Pick your favorite draft
                  To fill that mug --
             mmbb Maybe an dixm Alembic
             Mmgr Maybe a Dry-Hopped
                  The sweet bitter touch
                  Of a Hop Von
             Or if you want a bit more
                  Kick
                  Order up a Demo
             Then get some of the best food
             In all of West Seattle
        Strike up a conversation
             With Dan, Brian, or Jerome
                  Jameson or Silver
                  ttxfx Make a new friend
             Catch a smile and a quick joke
        From Suni, Lainie, Mikey or Maddie or Lopez
        Mikayla or Malia, Chris or Viki, Travis or
                                            Luke
             Or anyone behind
                  That friendly bar
             Then have another sip
                  And raise a toast --
                  Because you have already found
                       Your place.
```

TOP & BOTTOM: Elliott Bay Brew Pub, West Seattle, 2019

California Ave., near current Elliott Bay site, 1941

Lincoln Park

for Malia

Malia, who works at Elliott Bay, asked for a poem about her favorite place to walk and wander in West Seattle.

Lincoln Park old-growth Douglas fir, 2019

```
                    LINCOLN PARK
                     (for Malia)

Shhh
  Just step in
         And let the silence
              Take over...
         Let these old growth trees
              Whisper their history
         Let in these soft trails
              Tell you the stories
                  Of all who treaded before
              Thousands of years even
                  Or longer
         And wind your way down
              To the shore
                   Where those waves
                   Those skipping, rolling waves
                   Will let you hear
              If your listen
                   The sounds of
                        The infinite...
```

The Famous Maple
Fauntleroy Park
O.T.FRASCH SEATTLE 676

Fauntleroy Park cove and beach, circa 1908

Originally called Fauntleroy Park, Lincoln Park was acquired by the city in 1922. From 1931 to 1933, workers from Seattle's Unemployed Fund and from the Civil Works Administration (CWA) built the beach's seawall, along with shelters, tennis courts, and a series of park trails.

Slow Down

for Marcy

Marcy told the story of how, when she was a little girl, her parents were driving around West Seattle one day, passed by an older log cabin, and her mom said, "Slow down." They did, and her parents ended up buying and moving into the Log House—the current home of the Historical Society. And the place where Marcy grew up.

In 1902, West Seattleites William and Gladys Bernard built one of the first year-round homes in the area, the Fir Lodge. Constructed of local Douglas firs, it included a main lodge, stable, and carriage house. In 1908 the carriage house was relocated to its current spot on Stevens Street, where it served as a home for several West Seattle families, until it was purchased in 1995 by the Historical Society, who restored and converted it into the Log House Museum.

TOP: Log House, 1930s; BOTTOM: Log House, 2019; OPPOSITE: Fir Lodge, with carriage house in background, 1907

```
                    SLOW DOWN
                          (for Maxxx Marcy)

    Sometimes you just
       Know --
             Like when my parents
                Were driving by
             And said, "Slow
                        Fxxxx Down."

          And there it was
             Settled on the side of the road
                The log
                        House.
    And soon we were settled in
          Living our lives
                In those loghouse walls

                Trekking those short steps
             To Alki
          Soaking in the sun and water
             And just
                     Life
    Because this house
          This place
             Just calls
                Just whispers
                   Just beckons
          You to pause
             Slow down
                   And just enjoy
             The sweetness
                     Of
                        Here
                           And now.
```

West Seattle Life

for Isabelle

Born and raised in West Seattle, Isabelle asked for a poem about growing up on the Duwamish peninsula and still loving it as much today as when she was little.

Mom and child on Alki, 1910 and 2019, respectively

```
                WEST SEATTLE LIFE
                     (for Isabelle)

As a kid
  Those quick trips up here
    Maybe an ice cream cone
        At Husky
        Maybe playing hide-and-seek
            At Lincoln
      And even then, I knew
          This
                Was the place.

  And today
     Still here
        Still tasting and exploring
           Still taking in the sparkle
            From Alki
         Still walking those xxfyhix trails
            Of history
               Still watching those timeless
                 Waves and mountains
             Yes today
             Here
                  This is still
                    And always
                  The place
                         For
                            Me.
```

Coffee

for Nick

Nick DeJohn, digital intern at the Historical Society, asked for a poem about the PNW's favorite beverage. (Or, well, at least the one that tied with beer.)

```
                  COFFEE
                (for Nick)

The morning always comes
   Too early
      (Especially now
       In the 4:30am (!) sunrise summertime)
   And I am never
      Quite
           Ready.
      But
         Still
             I push up
                  Roll out of bed
         And then
                 Soon
      The air fills
         With that sweet thick scent
            Then my cup
               Fillstoo
         And then
            With that first sipr
                  Perfect sip
      I know that
         Just maybe
            And soon
            I'll be able
               To face
                     The world.
```

TOP RIGHT: Freshy's Coffee, Admiral District, 2019; BOTTOM: Nick with his poem at the Historical Society's street fair booth, 2018

Sunset from West Seattle water taxi, 2018

Nightowls

for Kerry

Kerry, a member of the Historical Society's board, asked
for a poem about her favorite creatures in the area.

NIGHTOWLS
(for Kerry)

Oh we are the ones
Who shine
When that sun dips down
When the darkness seeps in
That's when we come
To life
While others may slumber
And dream
We
Here in this shimmering
Soft darkness
We are the ones
Who make dreams
Come
Alive...

Illustration of Luna Park at night, 1907

To attract nighttime visitors, in 1907 Luna Park installed a "state of the art illumination" system, which outlined the park's rides and buildings in Westinghouse "A" lamps, considered to be the top light bulbs of the day. Ads promised "Brilliant Electrical Displays Every Evening."

Books

for Sierra

Sierra, a girl about seven or eight years old, said
her favorite thing about West Seattle was books.

```
                BOOKS
                    (for Sierra)

Just turn
   That page --
     Because waiting
         In those words
                 Are adventures
                    Are mysteries
                 Are journeys
                     To distant lands
                     Or just across the street

     Are people
         Who are nothing
             And everything
                 Like you

     Are wonders and worlds
         You xxxix never could
             Have dreamed
Yes take a seat
     In your favorite cozy corner
         Turn that page
     And begin
             The next
                     Great
                         Sixxx
                         Story...
```

TOP: Girls listening to storyteller at Lincoln Park, 1941; BOTTOM: Little free library near the Junction, 2019

WEST SEATTLE PUBLIC LIBRARY

West Seattle Public Library, 1910

New to West Seattle

for Jeff

Jeff McCord, a longtime resident and former president of the Historical Society, asked for a poem about being new to the area. As he explained: "When you think about it historically, we're all new to West Seattle."

Jeff: "The idea of being 'new' to a place is entirely a matter of perspective. This poem captures the realization that, in my own family's 25+ years in West Seattle, we would still be viewed as 'newcomers' to people who went to West Seattle High School in the 1950s and spent their whole lives here. And even more so to someone from their parents' generation, who went to movies at the now-demolished Granada Theatre in the 1940s. And what would the Duwamish people, who have been connected to this land for far, far longer, think of just 25 years on this wonderful peninsula?"

LEFT: Jeff McCord, 2017; RIGHT: Duwamish man and woman, 1904

"Birthplace of Seattle" monument dedication, 1905

```
                    NEW TO WEST SEATTLE
                       (for Jeff)
Me?
     Me I've only been here a quick
         25 years
       Just a decades and a half
               Blip
                  In our history

       Because there are those families
          Whose hillside houses
              Stretch back
                  Generations
       Who are were here
              When trolley cars
                  Ran down California
     And then back further
          To those who were here
              For the first Luna Park
          And those who settled
              At Alki
                  Before moving across
                  The sound

     And then
          Of course
       For four thousands of years
          xxxx Before
     Those Duwamish tribes
          Who treaded the tree-covered hills
          Fished the pristine sound
              Long before
                  Anyone else.

So
   How long have YOU been here?
          Yup I see you
              Are new too
          To this wondrous
                  Old growth
                          Gem.
```

The Future

for Shaina

While visiting her brothers in Seattle, Shaina Niswanger went to the West Seattle street fair, stopped at the Historical Society's booth, and asked for a poem.

```
                    THE FUTURE
                      (for Shaina)

What
    Is up there
            Ahead?
    Just around that next
            Corner?
        Will it be exactly
            Like you planned?
            Exactly
                Like you hoped?
            Or exactly
                Like you feared?

    NOPE.

The only thing
    About the future
        Is that it's unknown
    And that it's waiting
        For you to boldly
            Strongly
                Leap.
        Because it is that thrilling
            Stomach-churning feeling
            Of wonder
            That makes you know
                You are truly
                    Truly
                        Alive.
```

LEFT: Shaina at Seacrest Park, 2018; RIGHT: Young woman at Lincoln Park Pool, 1933

Shaina: "I chose the topic 'The Future' because I always worry about what the future holds and whether or not everything will be okay. This poem reminded me that I need to live in the moment and not worry about what is to come because life is full of excitement and wonder."

Old Growth
for Conrad

Longtime West Seattle resident Conrad Wesselhoeft asked for a poem about the old-growth trees in Lincoln Park.

Conrad: "Whenever I lose my way, or feel like a million scattered shards, I sight my eye up an old-growth cedar or Doug fir. I wrap my arms around it, lean my back against it, and feel the life within—the humility, harmony, and audacity. I like to think that something good and essential rubs off. It's my great fortune to live near Lincoln Park. Nearly every day, I follow a trail through the tall woods down to the beach. On a lucky day, I'll spot an eagle, otter, or sea lion—and on a truly lucky day, an owl, Dall's porpoise, or an orca. In some ways, time spent at Lincoln is the most important part of my day—when my worries are reduced to insignificance and my best ideas reveal themselves. Sean's poem captures an essence of this natural world, a place 'sunk deep with memories' and inexpressibly beautiful."

LEFT: Lincoln Park old-growth Douglas fir, 2019; OPPOSITE, TOP: Lincoln Park beach, 1901; OPPOSITE, BOTTOM: Conrad Wesselhoeft, Lincoln Park beach

```
                    OLD GROWTH
                      (for Conrad)
How do you measure
   History?
      How can you put a finger on
         Time?
      How can you encapsulate
         What it means
            To simply be
               Alive?

Well
      You can do worse
         Than trek down
            To Lincoln Park
      Where those trees
      Xxxx Are sunk deep
               With memories
      Where the Orcas and otters
         Swim with delight
            In timeless seas
And where
      Like this beautiful gem
      Of West Seattle
         What's old is always
            Sweetly
                  New.
```

With its towering old-growth trees, its meandering system of trails, and its narrow, wildlife-filled beach, Lincoln Park is one of West Seattle's greatest treasures. Because its dense growth leads right up to the water, the native Duwamish referred to the area as "Tight Bluff."

Murals

for Shanz

Shanz asked for a poem celebrating West Seattle's murals. She explained how she was going out and about the neighborhood, interviewing people for an ongoing project to save the murals, and doing a video for the West Seattle Junction Association, to help promote the mural restoration effort.

Shanz: "When you walk the streets of West Seattle, you can't help but notice the murals—the beautiful paintings on the sides of buildings, showing different historic scenes. After I learned of a project to raise money to restore the murals, I decided to do all I could to promote it. One sunny day, as I was walking around interviewing West Seattle locals, I came across Sean typing poems on California Avenue.

After telling him about the project, I asked if he could write a poem about the murals, as a sort of tribute to them.

"The poem he wrote captured the beauty, love, and respect for something so simple yet complicated, so historic yet current. Just like seeing the murals, the poem makes me smile, even gives me goosebumps, each time I read it—it reminds me that there are wonders on the mountaintops as well as the street corners. Words equal emotion. Paintings equal visual effect. It matters. The beauty of our area, whether natural or manmade, whether past or present, matters. This poem matters."

Shanz tipping her hat to Press Day mural, 2018

```
              MURALS
                  (for Shanz)

Oh sure
 Looking out
   From almost anyxx spot
Here in West Seattle
   You can see
        The most gorgeous views --
 Those timeless waves
        Of Elliott Bay
        Those green gems
        Of xx Vashon and Bainbridge
 And those towering wonders
        Of the peninsula
 But
        If you turn your gaze
           A bit closer
              To home
 You'll see those building sides
   Dripping and drenched
        With color
              And life
              And timeless scenes

   Because here
        Some of the greatest beauty
           Isxxxx also
        Wondrously
              Manmade.
```

Duwamish Bridge mural being painted, circa 1990

The Morgan Street Market mural (at Morgan Street and Fauntleroy Way) depicts a shopping center that opened in 1924. The center was part of the "drive-in market" trend of the time, and had streetcar service from both the Gatewood and Fauntleroy lines.

Morgan Street Market mural, 2019

Space Needle under construction, 1961

Space Needle

for Siena

Siena said she loved the Space Needle, both being able to view it from West Seattle, and of course to visit—to go up to the observation deck and see that amazing view.

```
                SPACE NEEDLE
                    (for Siena)

Oh it's a bit
  Of the future past
     What they imagined it would be like
        Decades ago
        That shining spear
          On the shore of the sound
        And yes
                When you zip on up
                   In those elevators
              When you step out
                   On that clear
                        Plexiglass
             (Do you dare
                   I Go all the way
                        To the edge?)
        Yes when you are up here
          With this view
        You can see
           How past present and future
                Merge
              Because up here
                   Is pure
                        Timeless.
```

Space Needle viewed from the Seattle Center grounds, 2018

Husky Deli

for Emma

Emma works at Husky, and said she loves it because the deli
has such history—and because everyone there always makes it
seem like a second home.

```
                   HUSKY DELI
                  (for Emma)

You walk in
 And it's like time
     Slows
         Like you can hear
             Taste and smell
           The history
              Of this wonderful city
         Where that scoop
           Of Husky flake
               Hasn't changed in decades
             Where those shelves
             Are still stocking the same
       Great fresh imports
           As always
   And where you can still get
     The best sandwich
       In the sound
   So yeah
       Come in this door
           Settle down
             Have a scoop or a bite
                 And feel yourself surrounded
                   By these happy faces
             That make this timeless place
               Feel like
                        Family.
```

ABOVE: Husky Deli, 2019; OPPOSITE: Founder Herman Miller, and his sons Bob and John, behind the
right-side counter, 1939

Originally started as Husky Ice Cream in 1932, Husky Deli has served scoops and sandwiches to West Seattle for decades. It added the deli part of the store in the 1950s, and has been owned and operated by the local Miller family since day one.

Youth

for Mikayla

Mikayla Ketner, a server at West Seattle's Elliott Bay Brew
Pub in her early twenties, asked for a poem about youth.

```
                    YOUTH
                      (for Mikayla)
This
   Right here
     This spring
       In my step
       This feeling like I
        Could just go
          Forever
    Bend and twist
      Runand leap
        Like I
          Am side-by-side
            No I am IN CHARGE OF
                 Time

    This
       This is the feeling
        Of pure strength
     Of that power
          Sweetly lurking
            Inside
    Of the magic
     Of me
    When
       Right now
         Here in this bright
           Strong moment
    Anything
      In my world
           Is possible...
```

ABOVE: Mikayla Ketner, 2017; OPPOSITE: Young woman at Luna Park, 1908

Mikayla: "When you're 22, you feel a lot older than you actually are. I chose the topic of youth to remind myself that I'm still young, and that I have all the time in the world to feel stressed about the pressures that come with getting older! This poem is incredibly motivating to me, and I keep it framed by my desk to remind me that 'anything in my world is possible.'"

Rush hour traffic, West Seattle Bridge Road, 2019

Traffic

for Natalie

Natalie, a reporter for King-5 TV, was doing a story on how the closure of I-5 that weekend would affect visitors to the street fair. So, appropriately, she asked for a poem on traffic. (King-5 then aired a segment about the poem and traffic later that weekend.)

```
                TRAFFIC
              (for Natalie)

Just when you think
   It couldn't get
      Any worse

Oh in a flash
Those lanes will close and merge
 And that traffic
        That seemed so crazy
              Before
Will move
    At glacier-like
          Speed

And maybe
   You'll avoid it
     Stay at home
        Or do something else
Or maybe
   Sitting there
     In that spot
        You would have zoomed right past

You'll see x that flower
   That perfect,
      Blooming bud
   That you always missed
         Before.
```

TOP RIGHT: Traffic at stoplights on SW Spokane St., 1957; BOTTOM: Most scenic way to beat the traffic—West Seattle water taxi, 2019

West Seattle Music

for Rebekah

Rebekah, a West Seattle native, wanted a poem about the great 1990s music scene that she remembered from venues all around the neighborhood.

```
              WEST SEATTLE MUSIC
                (for Rebekah)
If you listen
     Close
          You can still
               Hear it --
          Those twangy grunge notes
          Streaming from
               Easy Street
          Those unfound heroes
            Of the stage
                 Just belting it out
                    Here at The Junction
            Or up at Admiral
          Yup the heyday
            Of my music xxxxxxx happiness
                 Those sweet-sounding 90s
            That
                 If you listen
                      Closely enough
                 Are still
                      Playing
                           Strong.
```

ABOVE: Easy Street sign, 2019; OPPOSITE: Hamm Building, 1937

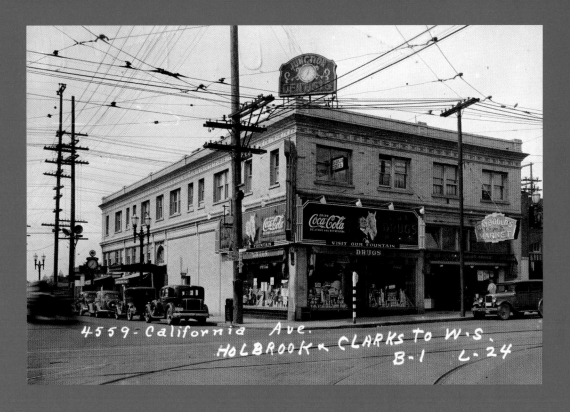

4559-California Ave.
HOLBROOK & CLARKS TO W.S.
B-1   L.24

Opened at the Junction's Hamm Building in 1988, Easy Street Records has been an influential fixture in the West Seattle music scene for decades. The independent store has hosted performances by local and national artists such as Mudhoney, Elvis Costello, Patti Smith, and Macklemore. Pearl Jam has enjoyed a particularly close relationship with Easy Street since the 1990s, including recording a live album there (Live at Easy Street) in 2005.

Caddyshack Tavern

for Aisha

Aisha asked for a poem about the Admiral District bar where she used to work. Alas, the Caddyshack Tavern no longer exists (the space currently houses the Mission Cantina), but Aisha recalled how it was modeled after the movie, with specialties like the "No Respect Burger," and plenty of laughter on both sides of the bar. And while the Caddyshack may be gone, beer-and-burger bars abound in West Seattle today, like WEST 5 in the Junction.

WEST 5 sign beckons visitors in from the snow, 2020

```
                CADDYSHACK TAVERN
                   (for Aisha)
       Can you capture
         The sheer whimsical
           Disrespectful fun
             Of the movie
                  Within Within a few walls?
           Well.
                Step on
                      Inside.

       And we'll treat you
           To a No Respect
              Burger
         We'll fill your mug
             With brimming beer
                And we'll fill your day
                  With just the right amount
                     Of fun
         Yup we will work
             Our asses off
              So that you can laugh
                    Yours off
                Here in these walls
                    Where life is like
                       A movie
                  And everyone
                    Always
                       Has a sweet
                          Good
                              Time.
```

Marty's Tavern at 23rd Ave. and Spokane St. SW (North Delridge), 1962; demolished in 1965 to build elevated West Seattle Freeway

Beach Music

for Amanda

Amanda's favorite West Seattle memory? Being on the beach at Alki during low tide and listening to the sounds of the tiny rocks and shells tinkling in the waves.

```
                    BEACH MUSIC
                  (for Amanda)

Turn down
     That radio
Put ꭤꭤꭤ down
     Thatꭤꭤ ꭤꭤꭤꭤ guitar
          And just
                    Listen...
Because when that tide
     Goes out
          The magic
               Comes in
     Those tiny
        Water-worn rocks
             Softly x tumbling
             Over one and other
        That timeless
             Tinkling
                  That
        Blended with the waves
             Makes up the ꭤꭤꭤꭤ music
                  Of
                    The sea.
```

TOP: Elliott Bay at sunset, circa 1895; BOTTOM: Alki Beach, 2019

Being on the Island

for Nancy

Nancy, who grew up in West Seattle, asked for a poem titled *Being on the Island*. "That's what me and my family call it here," she explained: "The island."

```
            BEING ON THE ISLAND
                (for Nancy)

Okay sure
   It's not technically
      An ixhx island
   But still
         Once you cross
               That West Seattle bridge
         That Duwamish river
   It's like the pace
         Even the traffic
               Just
                     S l o w s ...
         Where you can now walk
            To practically anything
      Get a delicious sandwich
         Or scoop
                  At x Husky
xixhx Catch a movie
               In old-school fashion
               At Admiral
         Or jaunt down to Alki
         And look
            (And maybe laugh)
      At the packed Seattle city
         Across the sound
            As you breathe deep
                  And relax
            Here on your ii island
                        Paradise.
```

TOP & BOTTOM: Construction of West Seattle Bridge, 1980s

Sunshine & Surfing

for Kelly

When she asked for a poem, West Seattleite Kelly Page said one of her favorite things was being out on the water—and riding those waves

Kelly: "My friends have called me Sunshine since our school days. Surfing and sunshine along with my yoga are zen and peace to me; the waves and sun are part of my being and soul. Being in the ocean with those rays shining down is my happy place.

"When I saw Sean at the West Seattle street fair, I asked him for a poem and he captured the sun! The words had me instantly smiling as it brought surfing, sunshine, and the ocean right back to me. My daughter and I walked off laughing, poem in hand; I cherish it and we have it up in our home."

ABOVE: Kelly Page;
LEFT: Alki Beach, 2019

Alki Beach, 1932

```
                    SUNSHINE AND SURFING
                       (for Kelly)

Tx The way those rays
       Sparkle and shine
           Along the waves
       The way that sun
          Happily skips
              From crest to crest
    Sailing and soaring
         From shore to shore
  Moving at the fxixfx literal
       Speed of light
    Oh yes
           When I am out there
              Just me and that sea
    I will try to capture
          Justa fraction
          Of that bright
          Sun-skipping
                  Brilliance...
```

West Seattle Commercial Club picnic at Colman Pool, 1947

Roots

for Anna

Anna said her favorite thing about West Seattle
was how wonderful it was to grow up here as a kid.

```
        ROOTS
             (for Anna)

It starts
  With just a few tendrils
    Those friends you make
      In kindergarten
           And then it deepens
           On their through elementary
             Middle and high school
   And the folks you meet
         At the PCC
              Or Husky Deli
         At the beach
              At Colman pool
         Or just on
              Your street corner
  And
        Kirk Before you know it
          West Seattle
                 Oh dear, West Seattle
          Has taken hold --
   And you
      Are forever
         Wondrously
                Rooted.
```

TOP RIGHT: Picnic in West Seattle park, 1937; BOTTOM: Family at Lincoln Park beach, 2019

Seattle

for Olivia

Olivia asked for a poem about all the great things in the Seattle area.

```
              SEATTLE
                  (for Olivia)

I can turn
  In any direction
    And see
        Beauty --
      Maybe those snow-capped
        Cascades or Olympics
          Maybe the mystical towering
            Rainier
      Maybe the crystal blue
        Of the sound
          Maybe the future past
            Of the Space Needle
    Or maybe
      These smiling folks
          At The Junction
      And always
        Wherever I look
            The sweet
                Safe feeling
                  Of home.
```

View of Seattle skyline from Seacrest, 1917 and 2019, respectively

THE SEATTLE WATERFRONT
PIERSON & CO Photo
© 1917

Space

for Gus

Gus, a little boy of about six years,
said his favorite thing was "space!"

```
                                SPACE
                              (for Gus)

            Oh up there
            In the starry swirls

            Oh up there
            Are whole other worlds

            Some parts are filled
            With inky pure dark
            Other parts alight
            With the tiniest of sparks

            And I as I gaze up
            I can't help but wonder
            Am I looking at the top?
            Or is that part down under?

            Because space, oh space
            Is all around
            Those sweet xixrax xf starry dreams
            From here on the ground.
```

TOP: Staring up from Little Si Trail, 2018; BOTTOM: Inaugural flight of the Boeing Clipper 314 flying boat, taking off on Elliott Bay, 1938

Star Wars

for Shannon

Not everyone had a favorite thing specific to West Seattle. Of course, many West Seattleites saw the iconic *Star Wars* films for the first time on the Admiral Theatre screens. And, with Boeing and the Space Needle nearby, and attractions like White Center's space-age Astro Park in the 1960s, West Seattle certainly has its link to galaxies far, far away...

```
                    STAR WARS
                  (for Shannon)

Some days?
     Some days I'm Luke
       Staring out
            With two-sun intensity
              At my future
     Other days
       I am Han
          Just going for the glory
              The gold
                 And maybe (who knows?)
                    Shooting first
     Other times I'm Leia
       Saving us all
          Or perhaps
            On those hangover mornings
              ⚡ Feeling a bit
                   R-2
                       Wobbly
     And yup
       Sure
            Every once in a while
               I slip to the dark side
            Breathe deep like Darth
               Hunt my bounty like Boba
     And then
       Other times
          When I just want to be
              Me
       I stand tall
          And let out my grandest
                    Wookie
                        Roar.
```

TOP RIGHT: Admiral Theatre at night, 1942; BOTTOM: Darth Vader sidewalk sign outside Hotwire Coffeehouse, California Ave. near the post office, 2019

Alki Beach

for Alyssa

Alyssa said she loved going to Alki Beach—all parts of it, at any time of the day.

```
                ALKI BEACH
               (for Alyssa)

Maybe I'll
     Start a nightime fire
       Gather round with friends
         And just watch the sparks
              Drift up
     Maybe I'll
       Join in a volleyball game
         Stretching and leaping
           In the soft sand
       Maybe I will stroll out
         At low tide
             Check out the xxxxx strewn seaweed
               Find that perfect
                   Elusive shell
     Or maybe
       I will just stand here
           And be --
           Looking out
               At those lulling waves
                   That distant Space Needle
               And just time itself
       Because here
         No matter where or when
             I go
                 It is always
                         Just
                             Right.
```

ABOVE LEFT: Alki Point ticket, early 1900s

TOP: Alki bathing pavilion, 1912; BOTTOM: Alki Beach, 2017

Douglas fir, Lincoln Park, 2019

Nature

for Emma

Emma, a teenage girl, said her favorite thing about the area was being surrounded by nature, and especially the trees.

```
              NATURE
            (for Emma)

⊠ What's the nature
   Of
      Nature?
   What if I could sit down
      And chat
           With that furling
              Fir tree?
   What would it tell me
      About life?
         Would it tell me
              How important it is
                 To have strong
                    Roots?
              To have thick
                 Skin?
           To make sure and get plenty
              Of sun?
                 And water?
         And how it's best
              To just go
                 With the breezy
                    Flow?

   Yup I think
      The nature
         Of nature
      Is just learning
         How to strongly
            Surely
               Keep growing.
```

Family in Schmitz Park, circa 1910

Gratitude

for Kris

When asked what was her favorite thing about
West Seattle, Kris paused, looked around, and
said: "This. Simply being here, now."

```
                    GRATITUDE
                        (for Kris)
    Just stop
        Here
            And breathe
                It all in
    Maybe you are under
      Some Lincoln Park old growth
          Maybe your feet
              Are in some soft
                  Alki sand
          Maybe you are just looking out
              Across the sound
      At those timeless waves
          Because really
              It doesn't matter wherr
                  Youxxxe
                  The best time
                      To appreciate
                  The wonder of now
                      Is always xxxx right
                          Where
                              You are.
```

TOP: Women at Alki, 1911; BOTTOM: Fence sign, house on Admiral Way, 2017

Death

for Lucia

When I asked Lucia, a little girl maybe seven or eight years old, if she wanted a poem about her favorite thing, she shook her head. "What would you like a poem about?" I asked her. "It can be anything," I added. In a serious, straightforward voice, she simply said, "death."

```
            DEATH
                 (for Lucia)

What is out there
    At the edge of
        The end?
    Does everything
            Go dark?
    Do you see
            A light?
    Or is it ᵼ something
            None of us can possibly
                Imagine?
    Well.
        You can ponder and wonder
        All the day and night
            About it
        Or
            You can realize
            It's out of
                Your hands
        And spend ᵈᵗ your time
            On simply being
                        Alive.
```

TOP RIGHT: Girls racing at West Seattle Commercial Club annual picnic, 1949; BOTTOM: Girls running the Pancake Flip Race, White Center Pancake Festival, 1956

Sean typing a poem, 2014

I Am Poem

for Tiffany

Tiffany said she was only at the street fair because her "Anthropomorphic Poetry" class had been canceled that day. "To honor that," she said, "could you write me something about a poem that's alive?"

```
            I AM POEM

              (for Tiffany)

This     paper?
    This paper pulses
     With life
       It is filled
          With tiny wood-pulp veins
       These letters
         Giving it shape
           This ink
             The life-blood
               Of me.
       Because me?
         I
           AM
             POEM

    I write
      I breathe
        I yearn
              I see the
        I am sublime
          And sometimes rhyme
        Yes me
            I type
                And therefore
                      I am.
```

TOP: Watching Sean type a poem at the street fair, 2018; BOTTOM: Children typing in Seattle, 1934

ian Totem Pole
Place West Seattle.
E. Standley

Admiral District
for Mike

Mike requested a poem about his favorite part of West Seattle—the neighborhood where he lives.

The first totem pole at Admiral District's Belvedere Park was donated in 1939 by J. E. Standley, the owner of Seattle's Ye Olde Curiosity Shop, and was likely carved by the Bella Coola tribe of British Columbia. Before that, the totem pole was located at Standley's house in West Seattle.

In 1966, the Belvedere Park totem pole was replaced by a replica carved by two Boeing engineers, Michael Morgan and Bob Fleischman, and stood until 2006, when it was removed for restoration and relocated to the Log House Museum.

The current Admiral District totem pole, erected in 2006, was carved by a Duwamish artist, Michael Halady, and was crafted in the traditional Duwamish "story pole" design. It is capped by a thunderbird that honors Chief Seattle. It was carved from a local cedar tree, using a traditional Native American crook knife.

LEFT: J. E. Standley, donor of the original Admiral District totem pole, 1925

Admiral Theatre, 2016

ADMIRAL DISTRICT

(for Mike)

It's like the crown
    Of the city
        The place where the two crossroads
            Admiral and California
                Join
    And also
        Where all different walks of life
            Merge
        Where you can get a perfect coffee
            Or her beer
                In the cozy Admiral Bird
        Where you can catch a movie
            In old-school
                Admiral Thx Theatre style
        Where you can walk up the road
            See the ancient
                Totem pole
            See the timeless view
                Across the sound
    And where
        If you're lucky
            You can walk a few blocks
                And be
                    Home.

View from Belvedere Park, Admiral District, 2019

The History of Seattle

for Oliver

Oliver asked if he could have a poem about the
history of the entire area, not just West Seattle.

```
            THE HISTORY OF SEATTLE
                 (for Oliver)

Let's go back
    A bit ...
        Maybe it's to those rowdy days
            At Luna Park
        Maybe it's to that vision
            Of the x future
                At the World's Fair
        Maybe it's to the tallest
            Skyscraper west of the Mississippi
                At Smith Tower
Or maybe
    We'll drift farther back...
        To those early settlers
            At Alki
            Switching shores
                After that first winter
And
        Even farther
            To those Duwamish people
                That have been
            That were
                On all the shores here
                    Way before
                        Anyone
                            Else.
```

ABOVE: Smith Tower, 1914; OPPOSITE: Illustration of West Seattle, Elliott Bay, and Seattle, 1891

SEATTLE
And Environs.

Over the years, Seattle has been a shifting mosaic, from the First People of the peninsula, to the early white settlers at Alki, to today's sprawling, crowded gem. Some pieces still stand, like the Smith Tower, the city's oldest skyscraper and the tallest west of the Mississippi when it was built in 1914. Luna Park, constructed across the water at Alki Point, was billed as the Greatest Amusement Park on the West Coast and had a storied (if also salty) history during its run from 1907-1913.

Love

for Ava

Ava, a teenage girl, walked up to the Historical Society's booth with a group of friends. Before I could even ask what she'd like a poem about, she said, "Can I have something about love?"

```
              LOVE
                 (for Ava)

You could sing
A hymn
But where would you even
Begin?

You could paint a work
Of art
But where would you even
Start?

You could look to the skies
Above
But what would that tell you
Of love?

Yes you can search for where
To begin
Or you can simply look
Within.
```

TOP: West Seattle High School, Senior Ball, 1914; BOTTOM: West Seattle High School, Senior Prom, 2016

For Malin, Who Just Turned Five

Malin's parents brought her to the Historical Society's booth and asked her if she wanted a poem, since it was her birthday. Malin was very shy, and hid behind her mom's leg. "How old are you?" I asked Malin. She held up five fingers.

"Would you like a poem?" I asked her. Malin clung to her mom's leg, unsure. "Maybe a poem about turning five today?" I offered. Malin stared at me for several seconds, then at the typewriter, then finally nodded yes.

```
                FOR MALIN
            WHO JUST TURNED FIVE

Oh there are so many things
      Out there
        Waiting!

Up ahead
      Just at the end
            Of this sweet summer
      Those first days
            Of kindergarten
And what what WHAT
      Will it be like?
            Fun?
                  Scary?
                        Better than you
                              Can imagine?
            Yup!
            All of
                  The above.
      And hey?
            Know what?
      Maybe at first
            You'll feel a bit
            Shy
                  A few bit
                        Unsure.
      But
            Just like today
                  Just like now
      When you asked for this poem
            Oh soon, Malin,
                  You will find
                              Your voice.
```

TOP & BOTTOM: Children on Alki Beach, 1921 and 2019, respectively

Seattle

for Maria

Maria said she was born and raised in Seattle and still loves it after all the changes—both positive and negative—she's seen it go through over the years.

```
                    SEATTLE

                  (for Maria)

A whole lifetime
   Here
       On the green
            Hilly shores
         Looking out
            Over those waves
         At those pnk peaks
            Across the water
         At that skyline
            That has constantly
                 Evolved
            Just like the city
                 Itself
         With the good and bad
            The crowds and if traffic
            The Space Needles and Smith Towers
                 Yes all of it--
                    Like the hills waves
                         And mountains themselves
                    Are what make this city
                    So imperfectly
                         Beautiful.
```

TOP: View of downtown Seattle from Elliott Bay, circa 1909; BOTTOM: View of downtown Seattle from Seacrest Park water taxi dock, 2019

1749 — WEST SEATTLE FERRY BOAT, SEATTLE, WASHINGTON,

Ferry from Seattle to West Seattle, 1907

Work
for Tori

Tori works in construction in West Seattle and asked for a poem about that—and specifically about women who work construction jobs.

```
            WORK
          (for Tori)
Yeah we are the ones
   Who get it done
 We are the ones
    Who make sure it's built steady
      And strong
 We are the ones
        Who put in the time
          And the toil
        And then take it easy
          Maybe with a drink
    Or just chilling
          With friends.
    Yeah we are the women
        Who work
 And oh
          Oh no
        Don't you men
           Even TRY
        And take credit
                  For us.
```

LEFT: PCC renovation, California Ave. near Admiral Junction, 2019

TOP: Girl Scouts at Camp Long, 1950; BOTTOM: Street rail renovation,
California Ave. at Alaska Junction, 1926

Lord of the Rings

for Chelsea

When Chelsea walked up to the booth, I noticed her *Lord of the Rings* tattoo, and commented on it. "Could I have a poem about that?" she asked. "About the *Lord of the Rings* books?" I of course said yes. And, while writing, I definitely pictured some of the West Seattle homes as cozy cottages tucked away in The Shire...

```
                LORD OF THE RINGS
                   (for Chelsea)

Yeah sure
    Going through the land
        Of the elves
            Is awesome
    And yes
        Riding to the White City
            Is sparkling
    And yup
        Even dropping that ring
            (Sorry, gollum)
        Into the fires of Mt. Doom
            Is the greatest
                Against-all-odds acheivement

        But
            For me?
    Oh for me
        Give me that Shire
            Those smiling dancing drinking
                Hobbits
            Those hillside round-door homes
                And the fieldsand flowers and food
            And just the simple pure
                Middle Earth
                    Life
            Yeah give me
                The sweet ▮ sweet Shire
                    Every
                        Hobbity
                            Day.
```

TOP: Colman bungalow, West Seattle, 1915; BOTTOM: House on Alki Ave. SW, 2018

Front lawn in Admiral District, 2017

Ernest Hemingway

for Holly

Perhaps inspired by seeing an old typewriter in action,
Holly asked for a poem about her favorite writer.

```
              ERNEST HEMINGWAY
                (for Holly)

 If this typewriter
   Could xxxxxxxxx channel him
     The way he sat there
       In his bungalow
     Sipping a drink
     Tapping out
       xxxx Truth
         On the keys
       The way he turned
         And told
             The tales of pure
               Raw
                 Humanity
     Knowing that always
       Someday
         That tolling bell
           Would catch up
           With him

   Yes if this typewriter
     Could channel
         That writerly greatness
         It would probably say:
             Not xxxx bad
               But
               Fewer words.
```

TOP: West Seattle High School book room, 1921; BOTTOM: Pegasus Book Exchange, Hemingway shelf, 2019; OPPOSITE, TOP: Hiawatha Field & Playhouse, 1912; OPPOSITE, BOTTOM: Kids playing soccer at Hiawatha Field, in front of playhouse, 2019

Soccer

for Sophia

Sophia, a teenage girl, said her favorite thing about West Seattle was playing soccer.

```
        SEE SOCCER
                    (for Sophia)

I am
    The wind.
        I am
            That flutter of breeze
            You feel
                    Coming.
        I am
            The air air itself
                In cleats.

Yes you
    Are going for
        That ball
    But you can feel it --
        The rush of me
            Sweeping in.

    And no
        You don't even want
            To turn
                    Around...
```

The West Seattle View

for Emily

Emily's favorite thing about being in West Seattle is one that all of us have undoubtedly been swept away by, at some point.

```
        THE WEST SEATTLE VIEW
           (for Emily)

Where else
  Can you look down a side street
    And be rewarded
        With a stunning glimpse
          Of the sea
          And faraway
              Islands?
    Where else can you journey
      Down to Alki beach
        And see Seattle

  As it was meant
      To be enjoyed --
    Across those blue-white waves
      Those giant shipping boats
        And the city skyline
        Buttressed by the spiraling
          Space Needle

    Yup where else
      Can you look
          ANYWHERE
          And see
              Magic.
```

TOP: Rotary Viewpoint dedication, 1976; BOTTOM: Westward view from SW Orleans St., 2020

86

View from the Admiral Way–Fairmount Ave. bridge, 2019

Acknowledgments

So many people helped make this book a clacked-out reality.

From very early on, thanks to the *West Seattle Farmers Market* for letting me set up my poem-typing table each Sunday.

Those market days led to lots of local support, including a "Whisky & Wine" event in May 2018 at the wonderful *West 5* (thanks, Mike and Sonja!) that brought me in touch with the *Southwest Seattle Historical Society*. Huge gratitude to *Jeff McCord*, the then-director, for the idea of having me set up at the Society's street fair booth that summer—the genesis of all the poems in this book.

Jeff was also instrumental in supporting the book idea from day one, and connected me with West Seattle historian extraordinaire and all-around nice guy *Clay Eals*. I can't thank Clay enough for his early advice, including leading me to *Petyr Beck at Documentary Media*. Petyr loved this book as much as I did, shared my vision from the start, and agreed to take it on as a labor of love. (Make money? Ha!) Put simply, this book would not exist without him.

Thanks also to *Tim Robinson* at Robinson Newspapers, for giving me access to so many photos and turning our coffee chat into an unexpectedly wonderful cover story for *Westside Seattle*.

In addition to Jeff, the rest of the folks at the Historical Society and Log House Museum have also been the best: *John Sweetland*, who sat with me one freezing March afternoon when the power was out, to find old photos; *Kathy Blackwell*, who got the board on board; *Tasia Williams* for early photo help; and the resourceful *Rachel Regelein* for finding photos even in the midst of the Covid-19 virus closings.

Thanks to *Julie Irick* at Seattle Municipal Archives, *Adam Lyon* and *Kathleen Knies* at MOHAI, and *Kris Kinsey* at UW Special Collections, who all similarly managed to find and scan photos when the virus was shutting things down.

And more and more, in no particular order: *Meaghan Kahlo* at the Seattle Public Schools Archives; *David Chapman* at www.otfrasch. com for the rare Otto Frasch photos (David is also Otto's great-grandson!); *Aaron Naff*, author of the wonderful *Luna Park* book;

Rob Ketcherside and his amazing Flickr photos; *Andrea Couch Wofford* for the gorgeous early designs that helped this book find its home; *Amelia von Wolffersdorff* for the final designs and layout that are still stunning each time I see them; *Jodi Egerton* and *Katie Sternberg* for invaluable input ☺; the staff and regulars at *Elliott Bay Brew Pub* for talking through ideas and making me love the neighborhood more each time I sat at the bar; and finally to everyone at the 2018 West Seattle street fair who took the time to stop at the Historical Society's booth, walk up to me and my typewriter, and ask for a poem.

—Sean Petrie, March 15, 2020

West Seattle Farmers Market, 2019

Image Credits

1: Courtesy of MOHAI, PEMCO Webster & Stevens Collection, 1983.10.6731

2: Courtesy of Brad Marcum

7a–d: Courtesy of Southwest Seattle Historical Society (SWSHS) and Jeff McCord

8: Courtesy of Sean Petrie

9a: Courtesy of University of Washington Libraries, Special Collections, negative no. NA1511 (E. M. Sammis, photographer)

9b: Courtesy of SWSHS and Jeff McCord

11: Courtesy of Sean Petrie

12a: Courtesy of SWSHS

12b: Courtesy of Sean Petrie

13a: Courtesy of MOHAI, 2007.39.50

13b: Courtesy of Sean Petrie

14: Courtesy of Sean Petrie

15: Courtesy of SWSHS

16: Courtesy of Freddy's Mom, Tiffany

17: Courtesy of the Seattle Municipal Archives, No. 66239

18, both images: Courtesy of Sean Petrie

19: Paul Dorpat

20: Courtesy of Sean Petrie

21: Courtesy of University of Washington Libraries, Special Collections, negative no. UW 40900 (Otto T. Frasch, photographer)

22: Courtesy of SWSHS

23a: Courtesy of SWSHS

23b: Courtesy of Sean Petrie

24a: Courtesy of SWSHS

24b: Courtesy of Sean Petrie

25a: Courtesy of Sean Petrie

25b: Courtesy of SWSHS and Jeff McCord

26: Courtesy of Sean Petrie

27: Image courtesy of Aaron J. Naff, *Seattle's Luna Park*

28a: Courtesy of MOHAI, *Seattle Post-Intelligencer* Collection, 1986.5.10200.2

28b: Courtesy of Sean Petrie

29: Courtesy of SWSHS

30a: Courtesy of SWSHS and Jeff McCord

30b: Courtesy of University of Washington, Special Collections, negative no. NA591 (Orion O. Denny, photographer)

31: Courtesy of MOHAI, PEMCO Webster & Stevens Collection, 1983.10.7430.1

33a: Courtesy of Shaina Niswanger

33b: Courtesy of the Seattle Municipal Archives, No. 29770

34: Courtesy of Sean Petrie

35a: Courtesy of David C. Chapman, www.otfrasch.com (Otto T. Frasch, photographer)

35b: Courtesy of Conrad Wesselhoeft (Bronwyn Edwards, photographer)

36: Courtesy of Shanz

37: Courtesy of SWSHS and Clay Eals

38–39: Courtesy of Sean Petrie

40: Courtesy of MOHAI, 1965.3598.2.6

41–42: Courtesy of Sean Petrie

43: Courtesy of SWSHS

44: Courtesy of Mikayla Ketner

45: Courtesy of SWSHS

46: Courtesy of Sean Petrie

47a: Courtesy of the Seattle Municipal Archives, No. 54247

47b–48: Courtesy of Sean Petrie

49: Courtesy of Rob Ketcherside and Washington State Puget Sound Regional Archives, King County property card parcel 338990-0115

50: Courtesy of Sean Petrie

51: Courtesy of SWSHS and Seattle Municipal Archives, No. 75033

52a: Courtesy of MOHAI, 2002.3.333

52b: Courtesy of Sean Petrie

53a: Courtesy of the Seattle Municipal Archives, No. 130331

53b: Courtesy of the Seattle Municipal Archives, No. 130330

54a: Courtesy of Sean Petrie

54b: Courtesy of Kelly Page

55: Courtesy of SWSHS

56: Courtesy of MOHAI, *Seattle Post-Intelligencer* Collection, pi21620

57a: Courtesy of MOHAI, *Seattle Post-Intelligencer* Collection, pi24611

57b: Courtesy of Sean Petrie

58a: Courtesy of MOHAI, 1966.3862.1

58b–60a: Courtesy of Sean Petrie

60b: Courtesy of Boeing Images

61a: Courtesy of MOHAI, *Seattle Post-Intelligencer* Collection, 1986.5.12594

61b: Courtesy of Sean Petrie

62: Courtesy of SWSHS

63a: Courtesy of MOHAI, PEMCO Webster & Stevens Collection, 1983.10.6779

63b–64: Courtesy of Sean Petrie

65: Courtesy of University of Washington Libraries, Special Collections, negative no. W&S 17682

66a: Courtesy of University of Washington Libraries, Special Collections, negative no. UW 40899 (H. Ambrose Kiehl, photographer)

66b: Courtesy of Sean Petrie

67a: Courtesy of MOHAI, *Seattle Post-Intelligencer* Collection, pi21617

67b: Courtesy of MOHAI, *Seattle Post-Intelligencer* Collection, 1986.5.16652

68: Courtesy of Brad Marcum

69a: Courtesy of SWSHS and Jeff McCord

69b: Courtesy of MOHAI, PEMCO Webster & Stevens Collection, 1983.10.901

70: Courtesy of MOHAI, Austin Seward photograph collection, 1980.6877.4.85

71: Courtesy of SWSHS (Jean Sherrard, photographer)

72–73: Courtesy of Sean Petrie

74: Courtesy of MOHAI, PEMCO Webster & Stevens Collection, 1983.10.9825.1

75: Courtesy of University of Washington Libraries, Special Collections, negative no. UW 1608 (Augustus Koch, cartographer)

76a: Courtesy of Seattle Public Schools Archives, PH 019-010

76b: Petyr Beck

77a: Courtesy of SWSHS

77b: Courtesy of Sean Petrie

78a: Courtesy of David C. Chapman, www.otfrasch.com (Otto T. Frasch, photographer)

78b: Courtesy of Sean Petrie

79: Courtesy of *West Side Story*, by Clay Eals and *West Seattle Herald*

80: Courtesy of Sean Petrie

81a: Courtesy of SWSHS and Seattle Municipal Archives, No. 31422

81b: Courtesy of SWSHS

82a: Courtesy of MOHAI, Colman and Pierce families papers, 2007.39.77

82b–83: Courtesy of Sean Petrie

84a: Courtesy of MOHAI, PEMCO Webster & Stevens Collection, 1983.10.2404.3

84b: Courtesy of Sean Petrie

85a: Courtesy of the Seattle Municipal Archives, No. 29286

85b: Courtesy of Sean Petrie

86a: Courtesy of *West Side Story*, by Clay Eals and *West Seattle Herald*

86b–87: Courtesy of Sean Petrie

88: Courtesy of Kelly Page

91: Courtesy of Kaya A. Hoffman

Front cover, left: Courtesy of University of Washington Libraries, Special Collections, negative no. UW 1608 (Augustus Koch, cartographer)

Front cover, right: Courtesy of Sean Petrie

Front flap: University of Washington Libraries, Special Collections, negative no. W&S 17682

Back cover and back flap: Courtesy of Sean Petrie

LISTEN TO THE TREES
A Poetic Snapshot of West Seattle, Then & Now

© 2020 by Sean Petrie and Documentary Media. All rights reserved. No part of this book may be reproduced or utilized in any form without the prior written consent of Sean Petrie.

Documentary Media LLC
books@docbooks.com
www.documentarymedia.com
(206) 935-9292

First Edition
Printed in South Korea

Author: Sean Petrie
Project Partner: Southwest Seattle Historical Society
Editing: Tori Smith and Judy Gouldthorpe
Book Design: Amelia von Wolffersdorff
Editorial Director: Petyr Beck, Documentary Media LLC

ISBN: 978-1-933245-61-4

Library of Congress Control Number: 2020938213

Author's favorite street view in West Seattle, westward from 45th and SW Edmunds, 2019